Forex for Beginners: How to Make Money in Forex Trading

(Currency Trading Strategies)

JAMES STUART

Published by BizMove
www.bizmove.com

Table of Contents

1. Making Money in Forex Trading

The Forex market has a daily volume of over $4 trillion per day, dwarfing the volume of the equity and futures markets combined. Thousands of people, all over the world, are trading Forex and making tons of money. Why not you?

All you need to start trading Forex is a computer and an Internet connection. You can do it from the comfort of your home, in your spare time without leaving your day job. And you don't need a large sum of money to start, you can trade initially with a minimal sum, or better off, you can start practicing with a demo account without the need to deposit any money.

Once you consider to start Forex trading, one of the first things you need to do is choose a broker, choosing a reliable broker is the single most critical factor to Forex success.

There are dozens of online brokers out there but your best bet is to go with the leader.

Based on our experience, The best online FX broker for beginners and pros alike is _____, to access it copy and paste the following URL into a browser: _____. Why? for starters this broker is rated among the best in trading quality, security, bonuses, payout and experience. More than that, _____ is much more than a simple

Forex broker, it is a "social network" that allows you to copy the trading strategies of the network's best traders (according to the company, over 85% of copied trades on e-Toro are profitable). You have to see it to believe it.

Now I would strongly encourage you to go and visit the above broker's site right now even if you are not yet decided whether you want to go into Forex trading. Why? because it provides tons of free education materials, videos and best of all a demo account that allows you to practice Forex trading for free without the need to deposit any money. Simply go to the site, register for a free account and start "trading" - by actually practicing and experiencing it firsthand you'll be able to decide whether Forex trading is for you.

In any case, before starting to trade for real, it is advisable that you practice with a demo account. Once you build some skill and feel more comfortable with the system you can start trading gradually for real money.

2. What is Forex Trading

Foreign exchange, popularly known as 'Forex' or 'FX', is the trade of a single currency for another at a decided trade price on the over-the-counter (OTC) marketplace. Forex is definitely the world's most traded market, having an average turnover of more than US$4 trillion each day.

Compare this to the New York Stock Exchange, that has a daily turnover of about US$70 billion and it is very obvious how the Forex market is definitely the largest financial market on the globe.

In essence, Forex currency trading is the act of simultaneously purchasing one foreign currency whilst selling another, mainly for the purpose of speculation. Foreign currency values increase (appreciate) and drop (depreciate) towards one another as a result of variety of factors such as economics and geopolitics. The normal objective of FX traders is to make money from these types of changes in the value of one foreign currency against another by actively speculating on which way foreign exchange rates are likely to turn in the future.

In contrast to the majority of financial markets, the OTC (over-the-counter) currency markets does not have any physical place or main exchange and trades 24-hours every day via a worldwide system of companies, financial institutions and individuals. Because of this, currency rates are continuously rising and falling in value towards one another, providing numerous trading choices.

One of the important elements regarding Forex's popularity is the fact that currency trading markets usually are available 24-hours a day from Sunday evening right through to Friday night. Buying and selling follows the clock, beginning on Monday morning in Wellington, New Zealand, moving on to Asian trade spearheaded from Tokyo and Singapore, ahead of going to London and concluding on Friday evening in New York.

The fact that prices are available to deal 24-hours daily makes certain that price gapping (whenever a price leaps from one level to another with no trading between) is less and makes sure that traders could take a position each time they desire, irrespective of time, even though in reality there are particular 'lull' occasions when volumes tend to be below their daily average which could widen market spreads.

Forex is a leveraged (or margined) item, which means that you are simply required to put in a small percentage of the full value of your position to set a foreign exchange trade. Because of this, the chance of profit, or loss, from your primary money outlay is considerably greater than in conventional trading.

Currencies are designated by three letter symbols. The standard symbols for some of the most

commonly traded currencies are:

EUR – Euros

USD – United States dollar

CAD – Canadian dollar

GBP – British pound

JPY – Japanese Yen

AUD – Australian dollar

CHF – Swiss franc

Forex transactions are quoted in pairs because you are buying one currency while selling another. The first currency is the base currency and the second currency is the quote currency.

The price, or rate, that is quoted is the amount of the second currency required to purchase one unit of the first currency. For example, if EUR/USD has an ask price of 1.2327, you can buy one Euro for 1.2327 US dollars.

There are so-called majors, for which around 75% of all market operations on Forex are held: the EUR/USD, GBP/USD, USD/CHF, and USD/JPY. As we see, the US dollar is represented in all currency pairs, thus, if a currency pair contains the US dollar, this pair is considered a major currency pair. Pairs which do not include the US dollar are called cross currency pairs, or cross rates. The following cross rates are the most actively traded:

EUR/CHF = euro-franc

EUR/GBP = euro-sterling

EUR/JPY = euro-Yen

GBP/JPY = sterling-Yen

AUD/JPY = aussie-Yen

NZD/JPY = kiwi-Yen

To give you a taste of what is happening in the Forex arena here are some historical Forex events.

One of the most interesting movements in the Forex market involving the British pound took place in the September 16, 1992. That day is known as Black Wednesday with the British Pound posting its biggest fall. It was mostly seen in the GBP/DEM (British Pound vs. the Deutschemark) and the GBP/USD (British Pound vs. the US dollar) currency pairs.

The fall of the British pound against the US dollar in the period from November to December 1992 constituted 25% (from 2.01 to 1.51 GBP/USD).

The general reasons for this "sterling crisis" are said to be the participation of Great Britain in the European currency system with fixed exchange rate corridors; recently passed parliamentary elections; a reduction in the British industrial output; the Bank of England efforts to hold the parity rate for the Deutschemark, as well as a dramatic outflow of investors. At the same time, due to a profitability slant, the German currency market became more attractive than the British one. All in all, the speculators were rushing to sell pounds for Deutschemarks and for US dollars. The consequences of this currency crisis were as follows: a sharp increase in the British interest rate from 10% to 15%, the British Government had to accept pound devaluation and to secede from the European Monetary System. As a result, the pound returned to a floating exchange rate.

Another intriguing currency pair is the US dollar vs. the Japanese Yen (USD/JPY). The US dollar and Japanese Yen is the third on the list of most traded currency pairs after the EUR/USD and GBP/USD. It is traded most actively during sessions in Asia. Movements of this pair are usually smooth; the USD/JPY pair quickly reacts to the risk peaking of financial markets. From the mid 80's the Yen ratings started rising actively versus the US Dollar. In the early 90's a prosperous economic development turned into a standstill in Japan, the unemployment increased; earnings and wages slid as well as the living standards of the Japanese population. And from the beginning of the year 1991, this caused bankruptcies of numerous financial organizations in Japan. As a consequence, the quotes on the Tokyo Stock Exchange collapsed, a Yen devaluation took place, thereafter, a new wave of bankruptcies among manufacturing companies began. In 1995 a historical low of the USD/JPY pair was recorded at -79.80.

The above started an Asian crisis in the years1997-1998 that led a Yen crash. It resulted in a tumble of the Yen-US dollar pair from 115 Yens for one US dollar to 150.

The global economic crisis touched almost all fields of human activities. Forex currency market was no exception. Though, Forex participants (central banks, commercial banks, investment banks, brokers and dealers, pension funds, insurance companies and transnational companies) were in a difficult position, the Forex market continues to function successfully, it is a stable and profitable as never before.

The financial crisis of 2007 has led to drastic changes in the world's currencies values. During the crisis, the Yen strengthened most of all against all other currencies. Neither the US dollar, nor the euro, but the Yen proved to be the most reliable currency instrument for traders. One of the reasons for such strengthening can be attributed to the fact that traders needed to find a sanctuary amid a monetary chaos.

Ask and Bid

When traders want to place an order on the Forex market they should be aware of the currency pair as well as the price of this pair. A Forex market price of a currency pair is denoted by two symbols, Ask and Bid, which have specific digital notations.

Ask price is the highest price in the pair's quotation at which a trader buys the currency, standing first in the abbreviation of the currency pair. Consequently, a trader sells the currency standing second.

Bid price is the lowest price in the quotation of the currency pair, at which a trader sells the currency standing first in the abbreviation of the currency pair. Respectively, a trader buys the currency standing second.

Seem complicated? here's an example:

Let's assume that we have the currency pair of EUR/USD with the quotation of 1.3652/1.3655. This means that you can buy 1 euro for 1.3655 dollars or to sell 1 euro for 1.3652 dollars. The difference between the Bid price and the Ask price is called spread.

The spread is actually the commission of the broker. The Spreads in Forex trading are actually very small compared to currency spreads at banks.

A term that you'll see a lot while trading Forex is "pip" and "pips" - a "pip" stands for "Percentage in Point". A pip is the smallest price movement of a traded currency. It is also referred to as a "point". It is very important that you understand what a pip is in the Forex trading because you will be using pips in calculating your profits and losses.. For most currencies a pip is 0.0001 or 1/100 of a cent.

When a currency moves from a value of 1.2911 to 1.2914, it moved 3 pips. When a pip has a value of $10, you have gained $30.

There is an exception for quotations for Japanese Yen against other currencies. For currencies in relation to Japanese Yen a pip is 0.01 or 1 cent.

Another term that you'll need to understand in relation to Forex trading is "Lots". A lot is the minimal traded amount for each currency transaction. For regular accounts one lot equals 100,000 units of the base currency. However you can also open mini and micro accounts that allow trading in smaller lots.

Understanding the Pip Spread - The spread is closely associated with the pip and has a major importance for you as a trader. As mentioned above, It is the difference between the selling and the buying price of a currency pair. It is the difference in the bid and ask price. The ask is the price at which you buy and the bid is the price at which you sell.

Suppose the EUR/USD is quoted at 1.4502 bid and 1.4505 ask. In this case the spread is 3 pips. The pip spread is your cost of doing business here. In the case above it means you sustain a paper loss equal to 3 pips at the moment you enter the trade. Your contract has to appreciate by 3 pips before you break even. The lower the pip spread the easier is it for you to profit.

Generally the more active and bigger the market, the lower the pip spread. Smaller and more exotic markets tend to have a higher spread. Most brokers will be offering different spreads for different currencies. Smaller accounts will generally have higher spreads than bigger regular accounts.

From the profitability point of view it is important to find a broker offering a lower pip spread, however the low spread is not everything. More important is to choose a reputable and reliable broker.

Most brokers will allow leverage. Leverage is defined as the use of borrowed capital, such as "margin" allowing the trader to gain access to larger sums of capital. This can heighten profits and losses and should be used wisely.

Here's an example: Trader A has $5000 USD – If Trader A has an account leverage of 10:1 and he wishes to use $1000 on one trade as margin, he will have an exposure of $10,000 in base currency ($1000) = 10 x $1000 = $10,000 (trade value).

Trader B has $5000 USD – If Trader B has an account leverage of 100:1 and he wishes to use $1000 on one trade as margin, he will have exposure of $100,000 in base currency ($1000) = 100 x $1000 = $100,000 (trade value).

3. How to Control Losses with "Stop Loss"

Stop loss is a widely used order aiming mainly at limiting the possible losses in case of negative market movements.

Stop loss is used only with open positions. When the market conditions are not favorable for a trader and the price has reached the level of the "Stop loss", the deal is closed automatically. Therefore, Stop loss helps the trader to control losses and in case of failures to keep safe at least part of his deposit.

If a trader does not use Stop loss orders, the position is closed by the broker when the sum of losses is equal to the sum of the deposit.

There are 3 types of Stop loss orders: fixed Stop loss, sliding Stop loss and combined Stop loss.

Fixed Stop losses are set while opening positions. They cannot be changed until the deal is closed. Sliding stop losses, on the other hand, can be modified any time depending on the price movement. Another name for sliding Stop loss is Trailing stop, that can be modified either manually or automatically based on the traders' settings.

There are many discussions on whether it is necessary to use Stop losses or not. Some traders believe that Stop loss is essential in trading, emphasizing the ability of Stop losses to prevent the loss of the whole deposit. If the price is rapidly moving in a direction which does not correspond to the forecast, a deal that has not been closed in time can result in a significant loss. The opponents of Stop loss believe that this order can limit not only losses, but profits as well. Since price movements are often unpredictable and unexpected, they can develop in line with the trader's expectations, though with some periodic bounces crossing the Stop loss line. In this case the position is closed prematurely with a loss while it could develop into a profit later on.

As a rule, the decision on whether to use Stop loss or not depends on the individual strategy and preferences of a particular trader.

Trailing stop is an order which its major function is to act as an automatic maintenance of an open position with continually shifting of the stop loss level depending on the price movement.

A trader may open a bullish position and sets the gap from the current price to trailing stop in pips. When the price goes upwards, the trailing stop follows it automatically sticking to the set gap. In case that the price goes down, then the trailing stop quote remains on the spot. In this way, a trader using a trailing stop has an opportunity to derive maximal profit at an ascending price with no regard to the set Take Profit value. Furthermore, a trailing stop is a loss limiter.

Here is an example: a trader opens a buy position at the price of 1.3400 and puts the trailing stop value at 50 pips back, i.e. at 1.3350. In case that the price starts to move upwards and exceeds the mark of 1.3400, the trailing stop follows it automatically keeping the set gap of 50 pips from the current price. That means, if the price touches 1370, the trailing stop shifts to 1320. If the price turns down, the price does not change its position.

As to a sell position opening, trailing stop behaves quite in the opposite. The trader sets it a few pips higher. At a price descending motion the trailing stop shifts according to the set size. With the up-going price, the trailing stop does not move.

While applying a trailing stop in Forex operations a trader will have to remove stop loss orders manually in line with increases in the trade profit. Trailing stop sets a stop loss level automatically at the value the trader needs.

A trailing stop is mainly used by traders who run trend trading, but can't follow the price moves continually. Trailing stop usage is also feasible at intraday trades, when quick reaction to price change is required.

Please note that trailing stops work only when the trading terminal is open. Once the terminal is switched off the stop loss is fixed at its current spot.

4. How to Use Forex for Hedging

Hedging denotes safety and security. Hedging means the protection of a client's funds from unfavorable currency rate fluctuations. Account funds are fixed at their current price through conducting trades on Forex. Thus, hedging helps to ease exposure to currency rate changes risks, which helps to prevent the risk of currency rate fluctuations.

As a matter of fact, hedging presupposes using one instrument in order to lower the risk related to unfavorable market factors impact on the price of another one directly associated with it. In most cases, the notion of 'hedging' means insurance from currency price fluctuations, assets etc. Hedging can also be considered as a type of investment allowing to minimize price movements risks in the market. The hedging cost should be valued with regard to the possible losses in the event of not hedging.

Hedging types in Forex

One type of hedging is protecting the buyer's money by lowering the risk of a possible increase of an instrument price. Another type is hedging the seller's money in order to lower a price drop risk.

Here's a hedging example: a trader, who imports in a foreign currency, opens a buy trade with the currency of his trading account in advance, and when the real time of the currency purchase arrives to his bank, he closes the position. And a trader, who exports in a foreign currency, opens a sell trade with the currency on his trading account beforehand, and at a the real moment of this currency purchase in his bank, he closes it.

5. Advantages of Forex Over Other Investment Assets

1. Simple to comprehend and master - In a Forex trade we deal with just a pair of currencies

2. Low Minimum Investment - The Forex market requires less capital to start trading than most other markets. The initial investment could go very low, depending on the leverage offered by the broker. This is a great advantage since Forex traders are able to keep their risk investment to the lowest level. Online Forex brokers offer "mini" and "micro" trading accounts with low minimum account deposit.

We're not saying you should open an account with the bare minimum, but it does make Forex trading much more accessible to the average individual who doesn't have a lot of start-up trading capital.

3. 24 Hour Market - Since the Forex market is worldwide, trading is continuous as long as there is a market open somewhere in the world. Trading starts when the markets open in Australia on Sunday evening, and ends after markets close in New York on Friday.

4. High Liquidity - Liquidity is the ability of an asset to be converted into cash quickly and without any price discount. In Forex this means we can move large amounts of money into and out of foreign currency with minimal price movement.

5. Low Transaction Cost - In Forex, typically the cost of a transaction is built into the price. It is called the spread. The spread is the difference between the buying and selling price.

6. Leverage - Forex Brokers allow traders to trade the market using leverage. Leverage is the ability to trade more money on the market than what is actually in the trader's account. If you were to trade at 50:1 leverage, you could trade $50 on the market for every $1 that was in your account. This means you could control a trade of $50,000 using only $1000 of capital.

7. Profit Potential from Rising and Falling Prices - The Forex market has no restrictions for directional trading. This means, if you think a currency pair is going to increase in value; you can buy it, or go long. Similarly, if you think it could decrease in value you can sell it, or go short..

8. No one can corner the market - The foreign exchange market is so huge and has so many participants that no single entity can control the market price for an extended period of time.

9. Forex is the largest financial market in the world - The Forex market has a daily volume of over $4 trillion. Such a huge amount of a daily volume allows for an excellent price stability in most market conditions. This means you likely will never have to worry about slippage as you would when trading stocks or commodities. The price you see quoted on your trading screen is the price you get.

10. Market transparency and Instant execution -
Market transparency is much greater in Forex than in
stocks or commodities, this means it is easier to analyze the
inner workings of the market and figure out what is driving
it. For example, economic reports and news
announcements that drive a country's economic policy are
widely available and accessible for anyone interested.
Whereas an individual company's accounting statements
are much harder if not impossible to obtain. Instantaneous
order execution is another great advantage Forex has over
other markets. Retail Forex trading is generally done over
the internet on all electronic platforms. The Forex market
has no central exchange and was designed to be this way to
facilitate large banks and allow for instant execution of
transactions, this means no delays for you and extreme ease
of execution.

**11. Price movements are highly predictable in the
Forex market** - Due to its highly speculative nature Forex
price movements tend to over shoot and then correct back
to the mean. This means there are a number of repetitive
patterns that are easily recognizable to the trader who is
trained in price action analysis. Forex currency pairs
generally spend more time in very strong up or down
trends than other markets, this is also a huge advantage
because it is generally much easier to trade a strongly
trending market than a chaotic and consolidating market.

12. No constraints on the number or type of

transactions - The futures market sometimes will have what is called a "limit up" or a "limit down" day, this means when the price moves beyond a pre-determined daily level traders are restricted from entering new positions and are only allowed to exit existing positions if they desire to do so. This is meant to control volatility, but because the futures market for currencies follows the spot Forex market the next day at the futures open their sometimes will be large "gaps" or areas where the price has adjusted over night to match the current spot Forex price.

Now, if you were holding a futures position over night it is entirely possible that your stop got gapped around, in which case you would get filled at the next best price, which often will be extremely damaging to your trading account. Due to the 24 hour nature of the spot Forex market even in extreme market volatility traders generally don't have to worry about gaps and can almost always get out at the exact price they want.

13. Direct participation, difficult to manipulate or influence - Forex trading operates in a decentralized online electronic market for its participants: Banks, FCMs, hedge funds, governments, retail currency conversion houses and high worth net individuals. There is no middleman between the trader and buyer/seller. Investors can interact directly with the market maker for pricing on a currency pair. Access is quicker and costs are lower than in other markets. Large market liquidity makes it very difficult for any one participant to manipulate or influence it.

14. Easier market analysis - Countries are more often stable than companies making it easier to predict their economic direction. Primary factors affecting demand and supply for Forex investment are interest rates and economic indicators such as GDP, trade balances and foreign investment. This and other economic data released regularly determines demand and supply for currency pairs.

15. Technology frontiers and investing - Technology enables the retail investor the ability to make better investment decisions through ready access to economic and political news events, to technical charting software and electronic trading platforms. They also have transparent and safe access to their investment funds in segregated accounts so that the safety of their funds is guaranteed.

16. Limited Risk - Despite the common perception about Forex being risky, it is easy to limit and reduce the risk if a trader chooses the right strategy. In addition it should be mentioned that stops are much easier to control as well, that is why newbies have good chances to succeed even while doing their first steps as Forex investors and traders.

17. No fees or middlemen - There are no commissions when trading on the Forex market. The retail brokers in this market are compensated through the bid-ask spread. Businessmen can also spot currency trading which eliminates the middlemen and allows each person to trade directly with the market that is responsible for pricing on a certain currency pair. Not only does this expedite the process, it gives each trader more options and versatility.

6. The Basic Forex Trading Strategy

The basic Forex strategy that is used by many traders of all experience levels, is Trend Following. This strategy is widely followed because of its simplicity to identify and trade and many times, strong trends can bail you out of an imperfect set of buy and sell rules.

A popular trading express is "the trend is your friend." This expression has stood the test of time because many traders find it to be a critical building block of a trading plan. Before we delve into the basics of Trend Following, it is important to first explain why trend trading is a popular strategy used by many new and experienced traders.

Do you have the perfect Forex trading strategy? I have not found it. To me, a perfect strategy is the one that wins all of the time and has minimal trade drawdown. I hate to burst your bubble but a 100% win ratio strategy does not exist.

Therefore, learning how to trade in an imperfect world is very important. Trend following is a simple way to cover up some strategy imperfections by identifying the strongest trends in the market.

For example, if the market is moving up in a strong trend, it isn't as important what the strategy is used to time entries, you simply need to be buying. When you trade in the direction of the trend, the rest of your trading approach can fall right into place. This doesn't mean that all your trades will be winners. It does mean that you don't have to be exact in your entries and exits once you find a strong trend to trade.

Now how do you know when a trend starts and when it is going to end? this is the $64,000 question. Since this is a beginners guide I will not elaborate on the various techniques that traders use to identify trends as this is beyond the scope of this book. I will however touch on several techniques in later chapters but note that these will be just in an introduction level without going too much deeper.

Any trader either a newbie or a pro should develop his own style of trading. There are several trading styles that you can adopt. You will choose your style based on your personality and financial capacities.

Many traders make the mistake of adopting a trading style that is unnatural for them. A trader may adopt one of the following two main trading styles: **Day Trading and** Intraweek trading. Let's discuss each of them;

Day Trading

Day trading on Forex means that one or few trades are conducted within one trading day. As a rule, the time intervals between the opening or the closing of trades may take from several minutes up to several hours.

Despite some difficulties of day-trading, this type of trading is very popular among the newcomers as well as among experienced traders. Day trading allows for the opportunity to make a profit in a short time with a small amount of funds.

In order to achieve favorable results in an intraday trading it is essential that you make the right forecast as to the price movement, as there are many external factors that cause high volatility in the currency market. So to make your day trading beneficial you have to track the market situation, collate facts and make conclusions about the price behavior of currencies, it is also important to be able to react fast so that you will find entry and exit points quickly at the opening or the closing of trades. Combining knowledge of technical analysis (to be discussed in a later chapter) with patience and observance a trader has good chances to earn well with a relatively low risk.

There are several strategies of day trading. The most widespread among them is Scalping - a strategy that is offering a fast opening or closing of several day positions. The trader closes trades while making just a few profit pips on each trade while the earnings come from the accumulation of a large number of successfully completed short term trades.

Another popular day trading strategy is news trading. Traders, who choose news trading, monitor the market events permanently, analyze the currencies behavior in different cases. Usually news trading requires an insight learning of market development and a proper trade experience accumulation.

Day trading can be a source of a nice income through the readiness to devote most of your free time to trading.

Now here are the advantages and disadvantages of day trading.

Advantages:

* doesn't require large sums of money;

* Trader may stop trading at any time;

* Minimal risk.

Disadvantages:

* High emotional pressure;

* Lack of time during a trading session.

This style is suitable for traders with endurance and quick reactions.

Intraweek Trading

Intraweek trade has no such furious market movements as in intraday trade. It may seem that the market is motionless. But it is just at the first sight. Intraweek trading has the following characteristics:

* A trade can remain opened for ten days;

* All trades are counted on taking the most part of profit

on market movement;

* As a rule, not more than 2 positions are opened during a week;

* Requirements for invested funds are usualy higher than for intraday trading;

* The work time is multi-hour charts.

Intraweek pros and cons:

Pros:

* Not too much pressure;

* High profitability;

* There is free time during a trading session.

Cons:

* larger volume of funds is required;

* Trader may be outside the market during a trend correction;

* Impossibility to stop trading at any moment;

* Necessity to hold opened position for 24 hours.

Probably, every trader can find additional styles, but the two that we've mentioned here are probably the most common.

7. Forex Trading Risk Management

Your first concern when trading Forex should be not to risk too much money on any given trade. Unfortunately, many traders start trading Forex without thinking about the risk that they are taking - only about the potential rewards.

If you want to succeed in Forex you must take into consideration the maximum percentage of the total trading money that you should risk in any one trade. Actually, your ability to limit your losses is equally as critical (or even more critical) as your success in managing winning trades.

The goal of practicing a good Forex money management is to minimize risk and increase payouts. For starters here are 3 quick tips:

First, Trading Forex is fun and exciting and money can be made; but you must also keep in mind that like with any other trading there is the risk of losing. Hence, Forex trading rule number one: do not trade with money you can't afford to lose.

Second, never borrow money while trading, trade only with your own money (this does not apply to leverage that is provided by your broker).

And third, set and stick to a budget. Write it on your forehead if you have to, but no matter what, when you hit that number, quit trading for the day.

Good money management calls for adopting a conservative investment strategy that means that you should never risk your entire capital.

When you enter a trade (no matter how great it may be), always ensure to only invest conservatively. Forex trading like any other investing is not a sure thing, there is always a risk factor involved. A conservative investment strategy helps you to conserve your money when things go wrong.

Forex trading offers a lot of choices to the trader. A good money management strategy requires diversification. The volatility that accompanies trading currencies is much distinct from say trading commodities as well as stocks. Obviously, the payouts may vary depending on the currency pair which is selected. As the saying goes, never put all your eggs in the same basket.

Losses in a trade should be accepted on a positive note. The effects of a trade that goes against you are able to impact the future or successive trade decisions. Expecting losses whilst investing can assist traders in identifying the areas which may happen to be unnoticed. Losses needs to be seen as a stepping stone instead of having it affect you.

Start off slow and scale up - this has a significant role particularly for beginner traders. Certainly do not fall for the emotions and commit your entire amounts right away on one trade. Investing in small amounts continually helps you to take a self-disciplined approach. The majority of Forex brokers allow for a small minimum trade sum. Use this advantage and be sure to trade with patience.

Do not expect to make gains with Forex trading as soon as you made your first deposit. No matter if you commit $200 or $3000 the exact same key facts apply. Trade in small amounts until you have the sense of the assets that you're trading. This can gradually build your self-confidence levels and helps to automatically be aware of the indicators and be able to prepare your investing strategy and ultimately help reduce the losses. One of the important things that specifies successful traders has to do with using a good money management strategy.

There is a fine line between gambling and trading. To 'gamble' is to take a high risk with limited chance of achieving your expected pay out. To 'trade' is to take a calculated risk which will nevertheless provide you with a good return as well as keep you in the game for the long run.

Not only will pursuing this kind of strategy truly enable you to improve your outcomes, it will as well help your mental well being. When starting any type of trading you shouldn't be in a position in which you are sweating on a contract winning.

Aiming and sticking with a strategy which offers successful money management does not just make sure you are not kept up at nighttime; it will as well make sure that a loss will not signal the end of your investing career.

8. What You Need to Succeed in Forex

Currency pairs are simple to trade but don't make the mistake of thinking that they are easy to make money with. There are many websites that tell you differently. They make you think that you just have to sign up for an account, start trading and ...voila, become a successful trader. Well, life is not that easy.

Like in many other areas, you need a solid knowledge before you get started. Hopefully you'll get some of it here in this guide. Be aware, though, that just reading this guide will not automatically make you an instant millionaire. You'll learn some facts and strategies about Forex trading, but in order to make the most out of this guide and become the trader you want to be, you'll have to adapt the ideas that you're about to learn to what you already know.

For starters you need to learn how to read the charts. Charts are your main weapon in winning the Forex wars - ...well, maybe I'm a bit melodramatic here. But seriously, charts are a vital resource for a serious FX trader, actually any valid strategy involves reading and analyzing charts.

Basically, the charts allow you to predict the future course of a currency by finding patterns in its past price movements, and after all this what we need to win a Forex trade.

Don't be intimidated by the charts, actually they are not that hard to read and understand. Strategies that are based on reading and analyzing charts are part of the technical analysis area.

Technical analysis follows a straightforward set of rules freely available on scores of websites. Happily, the simplest rules in charting tend to be the most reliable. In a later chapter we will go over several strategies that you can apply in your trades.

The most basic form of technical analysis would be to look for support and resistance levels that markets have struggled to break through in the past. Charts in this way works best in moderately volatile markets. Technical analysis is also useful in identifying trends.

Another simple way of using charts is to look at moving averages, such as the average price over 10 days. The idea is that this gives you a better representation of what the price is doing over a longer period of time.

Another simple pattern is based on the so-called relative strength index (RSI). This highlights situations where a market is overbought or oversold and warns of a potential reversal in the trend. The RSI is the total points gained on up days, divided by the total points lost and gained, multiplied by 100.

9. Technical Analysis As a Tool for Forex Trading Success

In order to be able to develop effective Forex strategies you need to understand technical analysis. This chapter is design to acquaint you with the basic terms and concepts of technical analysis.

So what is Technical Analysis?

Basically, technical analysis is the studying of investor behavior as well as its influence on the price action of financial instruments. The primary information which we have to carry out our studies would be the price histories of the instruments, along with time and volume data. All these allow us to make our predictions, depending on objective data.

Technical analysis keeps track of and analyzes the ways by which investors behave. This kind of behavior is collectively called sentiment. Technical analysts' viewpoint is that investor sentiment would be the single most important factor in identifying an instrument's price. Technical analysis practitioners believe that this analysis holds the real key to tracking investor sentiment.

In technical analysis we use charts to predict asset price movement and develop our strategies, this is why it is extremely important that you will be knowledgeable as to the various charts types that are being used in technical analysis.

Generally there are numerous ways to present price charts. Each has its unique advantages, however overall it is up to the person to determine which offers the best visual picture and is likely to be of most in discovering trends early on. We will look at the most widely used four types utilized by the pros:

Line Charts

This is actually the most basic chart format and is produced simply by using a line to join the data points.

The most typical use for line charts is for indicators that just have a single daily value (as opposed to high/low) for instance momentum or moving averages.

Here's a sample of a line chart:

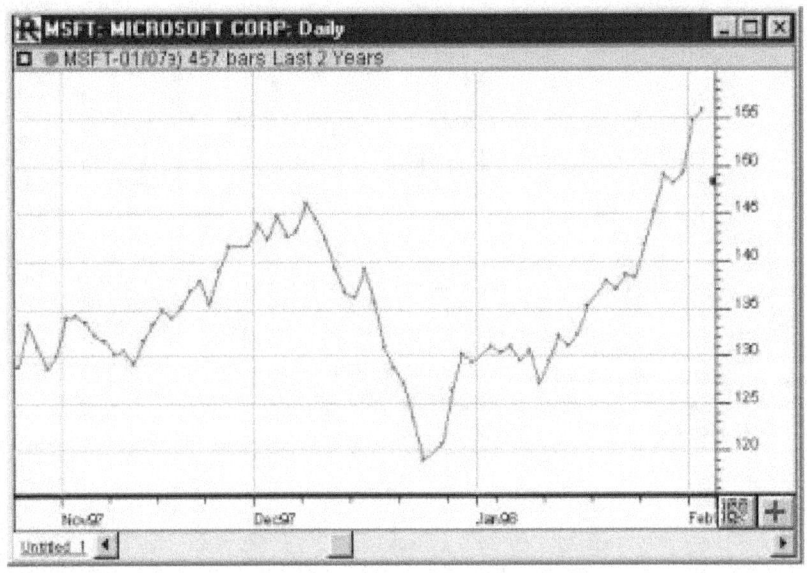

Bar Charts

Bar charts use vertical bars to show the price action of the underlying asset for a specific day, it indicates the lower and the higher price for the day.

As their name suggests, bar charts use vertical bars to represent price action for that day, drawn from the lowest price to the highest price.

Bar charts have indicators for the high and the low price of the asset. The left hand "notch" indicates the opening price of the asset and the right hand "notch" indicates the closing price.

Bar charts scales can be modified to show daily, weekly or monthly bars.

Here is a sample of a bar chart:

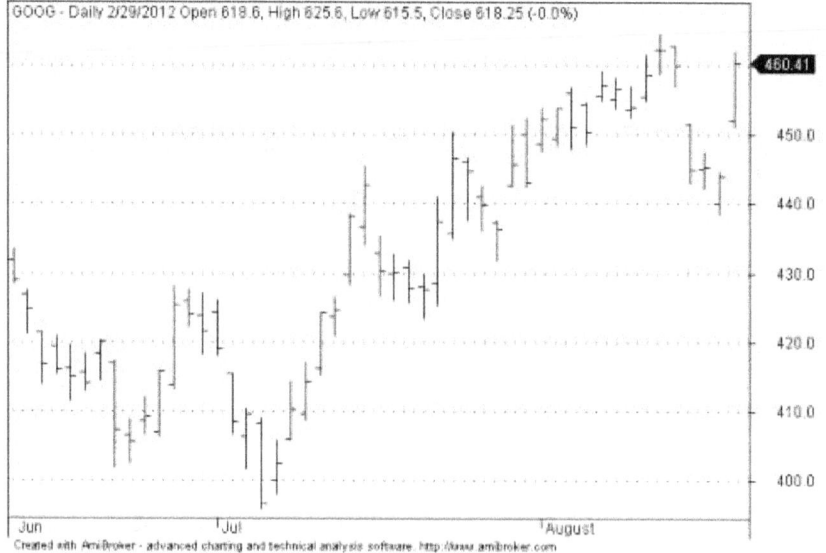

Candlestick Charts

Candlestick charts offer a more detailed visual representation of bar charts. The opening price is included in the chart and a day's activity would be represented as follows: an up day is indicated by a white (or empty) box. A down day is indicated by a black or shaded box. The "box" shows the open to close range. The "wick" displays the full day's range.

Candlestick charts are generally plotted over a one-day period but technical analysts also use weekly and monthly candlestick charts to provide a valuable picture of the longer-term price action.

Candlestick charting is one of the oldest methods of technical analysis, with Japanese and Chinese both claiming that rice traders were using candlestick charts over 4000 years ago. Candlestick appeal lies in its ability to give a clear visual representation of the price action during a period, leading to easy-to-recognize pattern recognition.

Here is a sample of a candlestick chart:;

Support and Resistance

Being familiar with the models of support and resistance is essential in creating a disciplined Forex trading strategy. Prices are dynamic, highlighting the ongoing change in the balance between supply and demand. By determining the price levels at which of these balances change we are able to plan the price level where to buy. Even though these levels could be created by the markets subconsciously they signify the collective views of the individuals in the markets.

Support represents the level where buying pressure is powerful enough to absorb and overcome the selling pressure. At price support levels buyers move into the market mopping up the imbalance between supply (sellers) and demand (buyers) so that when this happens the price will stop its fall and may probably rise.

Resistance is the opposite of support and is the level where the volume of selling (supply) exceeds the volume of buying (demand). These mini-levels may change frequently but over time a visible pattern comes out and firm levels come to be set up.

Here is a sample of support and resistant levels:

The Concept of Trend

We all know that prices do not rise or fall in a straight line but rather move in a series of zigzags which resembled waves. Now, the relative positioning of the peaks and troughs in these waves define the trend.

For a currency to be in an uptrend, it must make successive higher peaks (highs) and higher troughs (lows). For a currency to be in a downtrend, it must make lower peaks (highs) and lower troughs (lows).

Simply by figuring out these types of peaks and troughs, we arc able not just to explain the present trend and set it in its historic framework but, equally as important, figure out when it is changing. We do this by looking at the patterns created by the peaks and troughs.

Here's an example of a trend:

Moving Averages

The moving average is probably the most widely used indicator and is used by technical analysts for numerous sorts of tasks. Moving averages can be used to discover regions of short term support/resistance, to look for the current trend and as a component in numerous other indicators like the MACD, or Bollinger bands.

The primary benefits of moving averages is first of all that they smooth the data and therefore offer a sharper visible picture of the present trend and subsequently, that moving average signals can provide an accurate answer as to what the trend is. The primary downside is that they are lagging rather than leading indicators.

There are actually two major types of moving average:

The simple moving average calculates the average price

over a specific moving time period. For example, a 50 day simple moving average will calculate the average mean price from the last 50 days closing prices..

The exponential moving average also averages the last x days closes but designates a greater weight to the more recent prices which makes it more sensitive to present price action thereby decreasing the lag impact.

Here's an example of moving averages:

10. Developing a Forex Strategy and Entry and Exit Signals

The Forex strategies featured here are based on technical analyses. This guide is intended to serve as a primer and a starting point. To take full advantage of these strategies you need a level of technical analysis knowledge that is beyond the scope of this guide. However, you can easily find information online to complement your knowledge. Once you want to apply any of the strategies listed here simply run a Google search using the title of the strategy as the search term and you'll find plenty of information that will allow you to obtain the knowledge you need to put that strategy into effect. .

The Moving Averages Strategy

Moving averages gives you a hint as to the direction of the market, this is useful in identifying a trend. A trend is a good entry signal. A disadvantage of moving averages is that they tend to leg the market thus you need to use short period moving averages, such as a 5- or 6-day moving average, to reflect the current price action.

Moving averages are the most basic and most utilized technical indicator. They are used for smoothing the price movement. Moving averages are used as a trend line which adapts to price changes, not just as a regular trend line.

The Moving Averages strategy gives you the following signals:

If the closing price moves above the moving average - this is a buy signal.

If the closing price dips below the moving average - this a sell signal.

The Crossover of Moving Averages Strategy

Crossover of Moving Averages is another strategy that can help you identify a trend. This comprises of two moving averages: a "fast" moving average (e.g. 10 bars) and a "slow" moving average (e.g. 15 bars). The slow-moving average needs to use a larger amount of days than the fast one.

A crossover is regarded as a basic form of signal and is preferred amongst numerous investors since it eliminates all emotion. The standard kind of crossover is when the price of an asset moves from one side of a moving average and closes on the other.

Price crossovers are employed by investors to spot changes in momentum and can be used as a simple entry strategy. A close above a moving average from below may suggest the beginning of a new uptrend.

The Crossover of Moving Averages Strategy gives you the following signals:

When the fast-moving average crosses the slow moving

average from below - that's a buy signal.

When the fast moving average crosses the slow moving average from above - that's a sell signal.

Here's a sample of moving averages crossover

The Turtle Trading Strategy

The Turtle Trading strategy is quite popular among many traders, search the internet for explanations as to how to make full use of it. In essence, the turtles evaluate the high and the low over the past 20 days.

The Turtle Trading Strategy gives you the following signals:

When the current prices move higher than the high of the previous 20 bars - that's a buy signal.

When the current prices move lower than the low of the previous 20 bars - that's a sell signal.

The Moving Average Convergence Divergence Strategy (MACD)

The MACD strategy is another indicator that is useful in identifying trends. This indicator take advantage of the relationship between two moving averages of prices.

Most traders use the difference between a 26-bar exponential moving average (EMA) and the 12-bar. This difference is then plotted on the chart and oscillates above and below zero. A 9-bar EMA of the MACD, called the "signal line," is then plotted on top of the MACD, functioning as a trigger for buy and sell signals.

The MACD strategy can be used in various ways, however the most popular is to use the signal line for entry signals as follows:

When the signal line crosses the MACD from below - that's a buy signal.

When the signal line crosses the MACD from above - That's a sell signal.

The Williams Percent Range Indicator Strategy (Williams %R)

The Williams %R strategy developed in 1966 by Larry Williams. Its purpose is to help identify overbought and oversold positions in the market.

This indicator is categorized as an "oscillator" because the values vary between zero and "-100". The indicator chart usually has lines drawn at both the "-20" and "-80" values as alert signals. Values between "-80" and "-100" are interpreted as a strong oversold condition, or "selling" signal, and between "-20" and "0.0", as a strong overbought condition, or "buying" signal.

The Williams %R strategy gives you the following signals:

When the indicator has a value above 80 - that's a sell signal.

When the indicator has a value below 20 - that's a sell signal.

Relative Strength Index Strategy (RSI)

The Relative Strength Index strategy is yet another overbought/oversold signal. it was created by Welles Wilder.

The goal of the Relative Strength Index (RSI) is to determine the comparative changes that occur between the higher and the lower closing prices. The index is used by traders to determine overbought conditions and oversold conditions which then provides them with highly useful info to help establish entry points and exit points of the underlying asset. The RSI is an oscillator and its line 'oscillates' between the values of zero and one hundred. The values of 70 and 30 are viewed as significant values since above and below them are the overbought and oversold areas respectively. Just about any value above 84 is regarded as a very strong overbought situation and produces a 'sell' signal, while every value below 15 is regarded as quite a solid oversold situation and produces a 'buy' signal.

The Relative Strength Index Strategy gives you the following signals:

When the RSI crosses the 70-line, overbought-zone, from above - that's a sell signal.

When the RSI crosses the 30-line, oversold zone, from below- that's a buy signal.

The Bollinger Bands and Channels Strategy

"Bollinger Bands" incorporate a moving average and two standard deviations, one above the moving average and one below. The main thing to understand about Bollinger Bands is that they consist of up to 95% of the closing prices, according to the settings.

Trading Bollinger Bands can assist you to fully grasp a number of characteristics of an asset such as the high or low of the day, whether a currency is trending, as well as whether it is volatile or stable. Sometimes while trading Bollinger bands, you will notice the bands coiling really tightly which indicates the currency is trading in a narrow range. This is actually the trigger to look at for a price breakout or breakdown. Often large rallies start from low volatility ranges. When this occurs, it is termed as "building cause", this is actually the calm before the storm.

The Bollinger Bands Strategy gives you the following signals:

When prices move above the upper Bollinger Band - that's a sell signal.

When prices move below the lower Bollinger Band from below - that's a buy signal.

Here's a sample of Bollinger bands

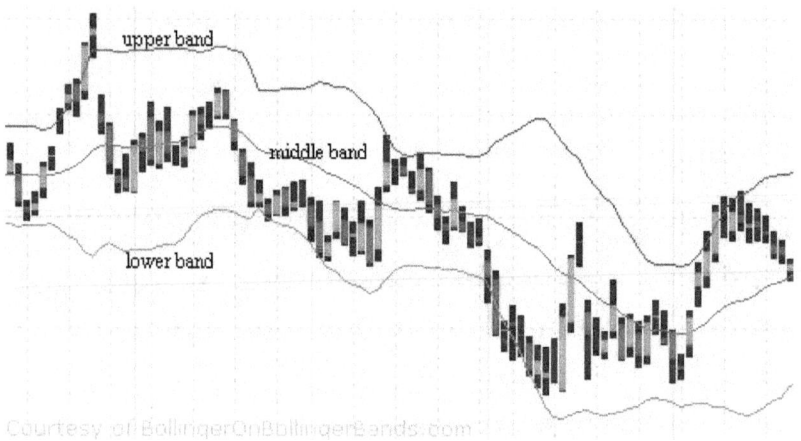

Courtesy of BollingerOnBollingerBands.com

Trading the News Strategy

The market is influenced by news events and by learning how to take advantage of these events you can improve your profits and prevent expensive mistakes. Many beginner Forex traders come to recognize the significance of news events only after seeing a perfectly profitable trade becomes a loss in a few minutes, while skilled Forex traders foresee the move and add to their daily gains in a regular manner.

Economic news reports usually initiate solid short-term moves in the assets markets which could create trading opportunities for traders. Announcements about corporate profits, a change in management, rumors of a merger, are all events which could result in a corporate entity's share price to move significantly up or down. Interest rates, unemployment and export rates, or the central bank's policy changes, can lead to a serious change of an exchange rate.

So how can you trade this strategy? simply follow the news closely and act fast. A good news event is a buy signal while a bad news event is a sell signal.

11. A Few Trading Tips for Dessert

1. Before implementing any strategy you must check for any related news events. why? because news events may interfere with your strategy and distort the outcome that you are expecting. Bad news may cause an uptrend to swing down and good news may cause a downtrend to swing up. Before implementing any trade simply run an online search to make sure there are no adverse news events expected.

2. Different parts of the day coincide with different amounts of volatility in the market. For example, the afternoon, when no major announcements are expected, will be associated with less volatility than the morning hours. Thus, trade volatility (Range Out) before noon and stability (Range In) afternoon.

3. You can expect the market to get volatile and make large swings right after major market announcements such as interest rate announcements by the fed and job reports.

4. Have a trading plan and a strategy and always stick to them.

5. Take time to improve your technical analysis knowledge, this will help you to sharpen your strategies.

6. Control your emotions and never trade when you are tired or drunk, this may lead to irrational behavior and losses. Always trade while you are relaxed and focused.

7. While trading, your main concern should be limiting risk and protecting your capital. Develop a money management plan and stick to it, always!

8. Define your entry and exit points. This is a part of developing and following your trading plan. Don't trade without having a trading plan.

www.ingramcontent.com/pod-product-compliance
Lightning Source LLC
Chambersburg PA
CBHW051249170526
45165CB00004B/1641